My Dress is Black, Never Red
A Financial Journey from Red to Black

Monaca,
Blessings to you,
LaKenya [signature]

LaKenya Taylor
"The Money Clues Lady"

Table of Contents

Chapter 1 Ms. Focuson

Chapter 2 Finally Home

Chapter 3 Meet Laura

Chapter 4 The Awakening

Chapter 5 A Glimmer of Hope

Chapter 6 It's a New Day

Chapter 7 Moving Forward

Chapter 8 Lunch with Lisa

Chapter 9 The Day After

Chapter 10 The Dress Arrives

Introduction

Thank you for purchasing my book. This book is simple and straightforward, but full of great "nuggets" that will encourage you and direct you into change.

In this book, you will follow Laura Focuson as she navigates her way through the personal and financial decisions we may all encounter, all while learning ways to embrace the valuable things in life.

As you read this book, you will be able to participate by answering questions and completing challenges in each chapter. Do participate and be honest. Change is on the horizon.

After reading this book, I believe you will be inspired, have a better understanding of your financial mindset, and be strengthened to leave the red and embrace the black.

Chapter One
Ms. Focuson

Nothing could ruin this day. As she drove to the boutique to pick up her dress—a several hundred dollar purchase that she could never even consider a few short years ago—Laura Focuson knew just how lucky she was, even though that "luck" was the product of an awful lot of hard work.

She entered The Little Dress Shop, an exclusive boutique located on Main Street, and greeted the clerk with a smile. "Hello, I'm here to pick up my dress."

"Sure, what is your name?" the clerk asked.

"Laura Focuson."

As the clerk searched for the order, another employee led Ms. Focuson to a dressing room at the back of the store.

The Little Dress Shop sold dresses from top designers like Donna Karan and Valentino Garavani. It was customary for their patrons to try on dresses to ensure a perfect fit, so a seamstress was always on hand to assist.

"This way, Ms. Focuson," said the employee as she led Ms. Focuson into a private dressing room.

Ms. Focuson entered the dressing room and gravitated toward the mirror to make sure she was still looking her best. She ran her hands over her black jacket and down her black pencil skirt. Excited to see the dress, she twisted in the mirror, checking her reflection from all angles as she waited.

"Ma'am, here is the dress you ordered," said the clerk.

Ms. Focuson was surprised to see the clerk holding a red dress.

"I'm sorry, but I didn't order a red dress, I ordered a black dress," she said, visibly upset. "I'd like you to reorder my dress. I've waited two weeks for this dress," Ms Focuson said in anger before mumbling, "I hate the color red, black is the color I ordered."

The clerk calmly asked, "Certainly, ma'am. Do you have your receipt?"

"Yes, I have a receipt," said Ms. Focuson, matter-of-factly, as she frantically searched in her purse to locate the receipt. "Here it is," she said, handing it to the clerk.

The clerk looked at the receipt and said, "I'll need to get my manager. Can you please wait in the waiting room?"

Ms. Focuson nodded. She was furious.

The manager came out and was naturally apologetic. "I'm sorry, but there was a big mix-up, ma'am. We truly apologize for any inconvenience. We will reorder the correct dress and overnight it to your home. You should receive it in the morning."

"Thank you, I appreciate your assistance," Ms. Focuson curtly replied as she swiftly left the dress shop.

The manager and some of his employees watched Ms. Focuson as she left, shocked that she did not threaten to go to the store owners or worse. Most of The Little Dress Shop customers were wealthy and would never be that lenient.

As Ms. Focuson walked to her car, she thought, "How dare they order a red dress!" She got into her recently purchased black BMW 5 series and slammed the door, enraged. As she left the parking lot, she began to replay what had just taken place and how she needed the dress in two days for a special award ceremony where she would be honored for her service within the community. She hoped the dress would fit right, but took comfort in the fact that she had shopped at The Little Dress Shop before and had faith that she would get her well-fitted dress the next day.

The Jolt

The light turned red at the corner of Timely and Elmer Street. As Ms. Focuson stopped, her attention was immediately drawn to a group of people who were picketing near the street, their signs informing passersby of impending layoffs and low pay issues. She was disheartened, as she had a great affection for people within her community. Some years ago, Ms. Focuson opened two community and job centers that provide financial management for families, grant classes for small businesses, job training for the unemployed and underemployed, and job placement assistance. From the beginning, Ms. Focuson worked closely with the managers she hired to ensure the people within the community were empowered.

Ms. Focuson also contributed regularly to Habitat for Humanity and other organizations in the area. Her philanthropy was not for recognition, but because the community meant a lot to her. She would never forget the individuals God sent to help her when she was in need, and because God had blessed her so, Ms. Focuson believed in blessing others. That's the reason she started the community and job centers, to help people and make their lives better.

One picketer limped into the intersection, just as the light turned green. He was scraggly looking, his clothes dirty and worn, a battered ball cap pulled low on his forehead. He dropped his sign, then leaned on the hood of her car as he reached down to pick it up. When he stood, he stared into the car, making eye contact with Ms. Focuson. His eyes seemed to scream "help me!" In that moment, her heart broke again. The picketer continued to cross the intersection. Ms. Focuson rolled down her window and called out, "Excuse me, sir, what company are you picketing?"

The picketer turned, a smile lighting his face, "Meager & Wilson."

"Thank you," Ms. Focuson said with a nod and a wave.

As she drove down the street she kept the picketers at the front of her mind. She was familiar with Meager & Wilson, and planned to do some more research on their business practices. Her anger about the dress was long gone; she now had bigger fish to fry.

Never Red: Questions and Challenge

How would you react if you were in Ms. Focuson's situation and were presented with the wrong dress?

_____

_____

_____

What issues are affecting your community? How can you help?

_____

_____

_____

Challenge: *Volunteer within your community in the next month. Try to volunteer at least three to four times a year. Check out www.volunteermatch.org for volunteering needs in your area. Get involved!*

Chapter Two
Finally Home

When Ms. Focuson reached her neighborhood, she couldn't help but smile, as she felt so blessed to live in such a nice and peaceful neighborhood. Everyone in Mapleton, Nebraska loved to drive through Lake Terrace Park to admire the stately homes, calming lakes, and scenic views.

Ms. Focuson finally arrived at her home, a lovely Colonial with immaculate landscaping. She was quite modest about it, but her home was once featured in *Better Homes & Gardens*. Ms. Focuson pulled into her clean and quiet garage, relieved to be home. She got out of her car, headed into the house, and jetted up the stairs to change clothes before preparing dinner. While in her large walk-in closet, she started thinking about the new black dress she would receive the next day, which would add to her collection and enhance her appearance at the Mapleton's Advancement Award Ceremony.

Ms. Focuson had a fascination with the color black—especially black dresses. They were her weakness, although she felt she had some discipline since she only purchased one per year. Tomorrow's black dress would make number 16.

Ms. Focuson headed downstairs wearing her favorite black jogging outfit. She didn't really jog much, but she loved comfortable clothing.

When she reached her beautiful kitchen, with granite countertops and stainless steel appliances, she sat down at the island and pulled out her notebook and iPad to quickly do some research on the situation happening at Meager & Wilson Company. She knew the company's president, Mark Meager, from a variety of community events, and he seemed to be a good, down-to-earth guy. She was surprised this was happening at his company. After a few minutes in thought, she called Mark Meager and left a message for him to return her call. She hung up the phone and continued further research. Once she learned more about the reason for the picketing, she decided it would be better to pay a visit to Mr. Meager to discuss his business practices and community responsibilities.

Never Red: Questions & Challenge

Describe your dream home. Do you believe you can obtain it?

_____

_____

_____

What or who has been hindering you from obtaining your dream home?

_____

_____

_____

Challenge: *Print out a picture of your dream home or something close to it and post it on your refrigerator, bathroom mirror, or in a place where you can view it daily. Thank the Lord for it daily and find a verse of scripture to declare.*

Chapter Three
Meet Laura

Ms. Focuson was indeed a go-getter. She was confident in every arena and rarely accepted no as an answer—a total difference from her younger days.

Ms. Laura Michelle Focuson used to simply go by "Laura," but now she requested that everyone call her Ms. Focuson because her first name reminded her of her past and always being in the red.

Laura grew up in a lower middle-class home where there never seemed to be enough money to go around. Her family's poverty was not necessarily due to a lack of earnings, but in how they spent what they made.

Laura's mom had a spending bug. Whatever she desired, she bought, which contributed to the family's predicament. Laura's dad was an alcoholic; after he spent the money he made from his factory job, he would take money from Laura's mom to feed his habit.

Even though Laura and her two younger siblings had a less than perfect childhood, Laura still wanted to be like her mom when she grew up. Her mom's life seemed fun to her, except for the part where her mom and dad fought and argued over money and his addiction.

Money Drama

Unfortunately, because of her parents' financial situation, Laura never learned to properly manage her money, so she was in a lot of debt. After she graduated from high school and went to college, she received her first, second, and third credit cards: a Visa, a Master Card, and a Discover card. She was very excited.

And she did exactly what she'd been taught to do: *spend*. She bought clothes, shoes, and more clothes. It was all so enjoyable until the bills began to flood in. She thought if she ignored the bills she would be fine. That did not work. Not only did the bills continue to roll in, but the collection calls did as well, sometimes in the form of threats. She didn't enjoy herself then. Stress became the daily routine for her. She changed her phone number many times to get relief, but that did not last long.

A major mistake Laura made when she applied for her credit cards was her lack of attention to the interest that would accrue each month. She was paying 19% interest on each card, which made her regret ever applying for a credit card in the first place. Laura even tried check cashing companies, which only drove her into more debt at a higher interest rate. Laura's life was certainly different than what she expected. She was the first to go to college in her family, majoring in business administration. Her financial issues caused her so much stress that she couldn't focus on her studies and ended up taking a break from school during her sophomore year.

Never Red: Questions & Challenge

Based on what you have read so far, jot down some thoughts you currently have about Ms. Focuson and what (if any) comparisons you see between your life and hers.

How was money handled in your home during your childhood and teen years?

_____

_____

_____

Do you think the way you handle money now was influenced by what you learned as a child? (Explain)

_____

_____

_____

Do you have a spending problem? If so, where did it start?

_____

_____

_____

Challenge: *Gather and track all of your debt. Use a debt app (like "debt payoff planner" or any other debt app) or put all information on a spreadsheet.*

Example: With the debt app, you can include all of your debt and each time you make a payment it shows you how much of a difference paying an additional $100 will make. The app also shows you how many payments you have before paying off a debt. If you use a spreadsheet, just include the number of months you plan to pay in order to pay off the debt. Let's say you have a $500 furniture debt and you want to pay it off in five months by paying $100 a month (you may need to update your budget to allow for this during this time). If you make the first payment in January, you will have the debt paid off by May. Once this debt is paid off, the following month take the $100 and either save it or use it for the next debt. Then start all over again.

Chapter Four
The Awakening

On Laura's 22nd birthday, she decided to purchase her first car. Not much was different, except Laura was back in school and would soon graduate. Laura was ready for a change, as she was tired of riding the bus to and from school and work. Laura thought, "It's my 22nd birthday, why not celebrate by buying a car?"

Laura went to Make a Change Car Dealers to purchase her first car. She walked the dealer's lot with a sense of excitement and anticipation. A black BMW caught Laura's attention—this was exactly what she wanted. She smiled and walked over to it. Behind her walked a salesman.

"Hello, can I help you?"

"Well, yes, I'm here to buy my first car," Laura replied, still smiling. "It's my birthday present to me."

"Great! You've come to the right place, and happy birthday!" the car dealer said. "Let's go inside to see what you're approved for."

Holding out his hand, he continued, "By the way, my name is Tom." Tom was tall and rather hairy, with a long ponytail. He was dressed in a nice shirt and tie, a crisp pair of blue jeans, and cowboy boots. Laura looked at Tom's hairy hand and paused before offering a quick handshake. The feel of sweaty hair was a turnoff, but she quickly reminded herself that she was looking for a car, not a date, and focused on the task at hand, her car.

Laura followed Tom into the dealership, ready to sign her name on the dotted line and drive off in her dream car. She was so elated that this day was finally here.

Tom said loudly, "Have a seat, I'll be right back."

As Laura sat down, she grabbed a pen from Tom's desk and began nervously tapping an impromptu drum solo on his dusty desktop. Laura's nerves were now getting to her and the questions began to roll. Laura thought, "Should I buy a car now? What makes me think I'm ready? Do I make enough?"

Tom came back in the room and said, "Let's get started. Laura, can I get your last name?"

Hearing Tom's voice and seeing his smile, Laura felt more at ease.

"My last name is Focuson," said Laura.

"That's an interesting name…focus on…very interesting," said Tom. "Kind of like you're 'focused on' buying a car today, right?" Tom let out an obnoxious laugh at his own joke.

Laura never had anyone dissect her name before, and thought it was odd, but went on providing what Tom needed to look up her credit information.

While Laura waited, she began daydreaming about what her friends would think when they saw her drive up in that black BMW.

Laura's daydream was abruptly halted when Tom told her that her credit was denied.

Laura was shocked. "How is this possible?"

Tom said it was due to her low credit score. Laura was very upset. Her dream just fell apart before her very eyes. This was her birthday and last year of college. She had just two months left before graduating from William Jewell College in Liberty, Missouri. What better time to get her first car? Dejected, Laura prepared to leave.

"Oh! Wait, Laura, I need to check on something," said Tom as he ran to the back.

Laura sat, staring at the wall, sad, embarrassed, and hurt. She knew she had debt, even beyond credit card debt, but she didn't think it was that bad. Laura thought to herself, "I will never be in the red again. I hate the effects of it. I will never be embarrassed like this again!" She made a promise to herself then and there, at Make a Change Car Dealers, to "make a change."

Never Red: Questions & Challenge

Have you ever gone to make a purchase and been denied credit? If so, how did you feel? If not, how would you feel?

_____

_____

_____

Challenge: *Get your credit reports and credit score this week. Before making a big purchase such as a car or home, make sure to pull your credit reports (www.annualcreditreport.com) and credit score (www.myfico.com) and do your research (you can also* *get a free credit score from www.creditkarma.com and Discover). It is good to be aware of this information. Knowing your credit score is like knowing your Social Security number—it is that important. It can be a hassle to purchase car insurance, rent a home, or buy a cell phone without a good credit score. If you need to increase your score, the best way to start is by paying bills on time. Also, check your credit report for any discrepancies. Discrepancies can drop your score. Selah!*

Chapter Five
A Glimmer of Hope

Tom came back to the office and said, "Laura, I'm happy to inform you that we do have one alternative. Remember, you're at *Make a Change Car Dealers*, where we make changes happen. We have special financing for people with low credit scores. I'll take you to that department if you're interested."

As Laura leapt out of her seat and followed Tom, a smile began to curl the corners of her mouth even though at this point Laura's hope was as small as the specks of dust on Tom's desk.

As Laura and Tom continued walking through the dealership, her hope began to grow. "Maybe I'll have a chance after all to get the car I want, that beautiful black BMW," she thought.

Tom led Laura to an office across the car lot where he introduced her to the finance officer. "Laura, this is Chris."

Chris held out his hand for Laura to shake, "Hi, Laura, I'm one of Make a Change's special financing consultants. Please have a seat."

"Alright, Laura, I'm going to leave you in Chris's hands," said Tom as he walked away with a big smile.

Laura smiled at Tom and then turned her attention to Chris to see what he could do.

Chris seemed very mild-mannered in comparison to Tom, and he was a lot less hairy. Tom was loud, laughed at his own jokes, and walked real fast, as if he always had somewhere else to be.

Chris had red hair, a soft smile, and great teeth. As Laura looked at Chris, she realized she was back in another decision room, regardless of how nice Chris looked or spoke. Her knees began to knock in anticipation of what Chris would say next.

Chris kept his eyes on the computer, typed some, looked at his paperwork, and then back at the computer. "Well, Laura, we have good news: We got you approved," said Chris.

Laura's eyes began to light up, until Chris continued, "But the only thing we have that will fit your situation is a 1992 Honda Civic. It isn't fancy, but it's a good, reliable little car. Would you like to take a look?" he asked.

"Uh, I guess so," said Laura, dejectedly. This definitely was not the kind of car she had in mind. She was extremely disappointed in not being able to get the black BMW, but she wanted to stay positive.

The Answer

Chris called Tom back to the room.

Tom smiled. "Well, it looks like you got approved and Chris found you a car, let's go have a look!"

Laura slowly got up from the chair and followed Tom as he walked swiftly to the front door to open it for her. Tom had a wide smile on his face, as if Laura was going to see her dream car. Laura's head was tilted down. She was led by the jangling of the keys in Tom's hand.

Tom and Laura passed the black BMW that Laura wanted and then passed a few other options that would have fit Laura's desires. Tom turned and began walking toward a beautiful, nice, shiny black car, and Laura's head began to rise higher.

Alas, it was a false alarm! Tom made a quick shift to the right, away from that beauty, and said, "Here we are. What do you think?"

Laura was not happy. The car was red. That was the ultimate issue. She didn't want a red car because she just mentioned that she would never be in the red again and a red car would represent that. The car was not only red, but it was a small, two-door car with manual windows and locks. Not an exciting car at all!

"How about you take a test drive?"

"Um, I guess so," Laura said as she gingerly took the keys from Tom. Laura got in the car slowly, looking around as if it was straight out of a scary movie. The red car had basic cloth seats and a bit of a funky smell.

Laura started up the car and flinched as she heard what sounded like a lawnmower passing her by. Actually, it was just the roar of the car's tiny engine coming to life. Laura drove off the lot and wondered to herself, "What am I doing? Why am I in this car? I need a car, but this one is red, stinky, loud, and just not me." She continued to wrestle in her mind with what to do.

Laura knew she needed a car, but this was not the car she wanted; still she had a decision to make.

Laura didn't want to call her parents, and her siblings were too young to offer advice. "Do I not get the car—the only car that I'm approved for—because of my ego or do I get the car that will allow me to get to work without taking the bus or asking a friend?" Laura whispered.

    Laura thought for a moment as tears began to well up in her eyes, but she had to lay down her pride. Laura pulled back into the dealership, her decision made. Tom ran toward the car as Laura stopped.

    "How was the drive?" he asked.

    With a big sigh, Laura straightened her stooped shoulders, cleared her throat and said, "I'll take it."

    "Are you sure?" Tom asked.

    Again clearing her throat, Laura responded, "Yes, I am." She tried to smile but failed miserably.

    "Great, let's draw up the paperwork," replied Tom, rubbing his hands.

The Next Phase

"So, are you sure this is the only color you have in this make?" Laura asked as they headed back in the dealership office,

Laughing, Tom said, "Yes, but the way the special financing program works is if you make your payments on time for nine months, you can come back and possibly qualify for a different vehicle."

Laura felt a lot better after hearing this news, as she hated the color red and wasn't thrilled about the car either. She sat down with Tom and Chris, listening to them, as they went over terms and interest. Laura then perused each document they placed before her. It took a while, but Laura was soon in a groove.

After signing all the documents, she shook hands with Tom and Chris, and was given her keys.

Laura signed a loan with *Make a Change Car Dealership* at 22% interest. The car cost $10,000 and with the interest and fees, her monthly car payments totaled $303.20.

Never Red: Questions & Challenge

Do you think Laura made the right decision to purchase the car? Was there a way Laura could have gotten the interest down?

_____

_____

_____

Have you ever experienced a situation like Laura's, not getting the car you wanted or something else you wanted? If so, how did you handle it? If not, how would you have handled not getting what you wanted?

_____

_____

_____

Challenge: *Always do your research before making any major purchase. This includes appliances, a vehicle, home, computer, and other important items. Start researching now for future purchases.*

Chapter Six
It's a New Day

Laura got in her new car thinking, "I can do this. I can pay on time for nine months and get a better car, a black car." When Laura drove off the lot of Make a Change Dealers, she realized she had an eye-opening experience. She knew at that moment she would have to do something different. It was time to "make a change" anyway. Laura was so stressed that while driving she started to cry, blubbering, "I'm in the red. I don't want to be in the red. I'm even in a red car."

Laura made up in her mind at that moment to start paying down her debts. She promised herself that she would never be in the "red" again and neither would her future children. Her red car would remind her of her debt, Laura decided. She would see it as a means to push herself out of debt because she hated the color red and the financial meaning behind it.

The Dilemma: Making the First On-Time Payment

Laura had been a faithful employee at the college's food court and at her part-time job at the town's movie theatre. She was making decent money for a college student and soon-to-be graduate.

Laura knew that after she graduated from William Jewell College, she wanted to live and work in St. Louis, so she sent resumes to several companies there and landed a couple of interviews. The day she got her first car loan statement was the same day she received an email from Red Kirk Business Solutions, a prestigious company located in St. Louis. Laura had interviewed for a position a few weeks before and received an offer for an operations analyst position. Laura was excited about the offer, but hesitant about the company's name and about her car loan statement. "Really, Red Kirk?" Laura asked herself, flustered by her seeming inability to escape the color red. She thought about the commitment she made to pay her bills on time and how she had not kept her word. "This isn't a joke, this is for real. I have a job offer. Will I succeed or not?" These thoughts constantly ran through Laura's head. All she knew was she had to make a real change because her debts were piling up. And now with a possible good job, would it be easier to pay them off or would she dig herself deeper into debt?

The company gave her a great offer plus awesome benefits. Laura emailed the company and accepted the job with a salary of $35,000 a year and requested to begin in a month, after graduation. The company agreed.

After Laura graduated, she was ready to move. Fortunately, her parents were able to help her by paying her moving expenses to St. Louis, as well as her deposit and first month's rent on a one-bedroom apartment.

She moved to the Creve Coeur area, a nice suburb of St. Louis. Laura was glad to be in such a nice area, but her apartment seemed out of place as it was old, with green carpet, flowery wallpaper, and a bathroom door that creaked loudly.

Laura was a little nervous about the place, but tried to focus on her good-paying job and reaching her goals. While Laura was unpacking she ran across her car loan statement. She'd forgotten about it, as she was so excited about the new job. She had three days left to pay before the payment would be late.

Laura had the money, but really wanted to decorate her new apartment so it would look somewhat livable. "Oh, darn! I want to enjoy my new life," said Laura with great frustration as she threw the statement on the floor and went to grab more boxes.

Laura spent the rest of the day moving things in from her car. As she ran down the steps from her third-floor apartment to get the last load from her car, her eyes focused on that red 1992 Honda that she bought a little over two months ago. "Gee whiz, I don't like that color," she thought.

"If I don't make the payment, will I lose my only form of transportation?" she wondered. Laura stopped thinking about what she wanted and instead concentrated on what she needed. She remembered her thoughts about the car not looking the best while taking the test drive. She could not turn back but move forward. The car was not the greatest but had been reliable thus far. She needed to pay her car note.

Laura turned around and ran back into her apartment, threw her last box down, opened her laptop, went to the finance company's website, provided her bank account information and made her first on-time payment of $303.20. Laura felt so relieved. She paid for something on time for the first time in her life. Laura knew then she could do it. Laura was on her way to real change.

The New Job

The next day, Laura began her new job. She was so excited. She didn't have much money left since she paid her car note, but was ready to get to work and make money. When she arrived, she was welcomed by Mr. George Perry, the manager of the operations department. He was a well-dressed, clean-cut man. He wore Laura's favorite male cologne, Polo. She was in love.

"Welcome to your place of change," said Mr. Perry with a smile on his face.

Laura thought his welcome was quite odd but smiled and decided not to comment. As he gave her a tour of the department, she kept trying to figure out what exactly his welcome meant. It was a hard one to wrap her mind around, so she pushed it to the back of her mind to review later.

At the end of the tour, Mr. Perry stopped and gestured toward a small enclosed space. "Here is your cubicle," he said. Laura looked at her office space. She couldn't believe it, no more standing on her feet all day flipping burgers or taking customers' movie tickets. She was finally going to be able to sit down and rest her feet. It was a cubicle, but it was just the right size for Laura; she didn't have much to fill it with, anyway.

Excited about her very own cubicle, Laura was looking through her drawers when a soft voice asked, "Hi, are you making yourself at home?"

Laura looked up to see Regina White, the assistant manager of the operations department. Mr. Perry pointed Ms. White out during Laura's tour, but they were not introduced. Ms. White had a bright and peaceful smile and wore a black professional dress with black stilettos.

"Yes, I am," Laura replied.

"Good. I'm Ms. White, assistant manager of operations," she said. "I'm here if you need anything. I have an open-door policy, so feel free to come see me anytime."

"Thanks," said Laura.

As Laura met her many coworkers, she was so impressed with how people dressed in her department and within the company in general. Laura had on a blue suit jacket from Goodwill, with a white tank, black slacks, and black shoes from Payless. After seeing how everyone else dressed, Laura thought she should step it up a bit and buy fancier clothes. Of course, to do this she would have to use her credit cards, which all were maxed out except for one that was close to the limit. Not a good idea, but Laura wanted to "keep up with the Joneses," as one would say.

Laura decided to go shopping at the West County Mall after work. She could not wait to get there. After work, she said goodbye to everyone she met in her department as well as the receptionist at the front desk. Off she went to the mall as if she were following the yellow brick road to the Land of Oz. As Laura drove down the highway, reality set in.

"What am I doing?" she whispered. "I am already over $20,000 in debt. I have credit card debt, student loans to pay, a car note, rent, utilities, and the list goes on." Really hit Laura that day. She realized she had a major problem and it was time to truly make a change.

Laura got off at the next exit and instead of going to the mall, she went home. While driving home, Laura thought about her issues and began to ask questions. "Where did this habit come from? Why am I like this? What is driving me to want to spend so that I am in bondage to it instead of being financially free? What changes do I need to make?" Laura believed in prayer, so she prayed and asked God to help her.

When Laura got home, she took out a piece of paper and wrote down the questions she had asked while driving home and began to answer them. It was as if she knew the answers all along.

Where did my spending habit come from? *This is a learned behavior from my parents. They spent money all the time on unnecessary things.*

Why am I like this? *I thought what I was doing was the only way of life. I never broke the cycle by educating myself or attempted to do anything different.*

What is driving me to want to spend so that I am in bondage to debt instead of being financially free? *I lack financial literacy. I keep taking the bait that keeps me in debt, and I lack the drive to be debt-free. I focus on my wants more than needs.*

What changes do I need to make? *Have a budget, be educated financially, and don't stop.*

After Laura answered her four questions, she pondered her answers then decided to create a budget in Microsoft Excel and to educate herself.

The next day Laura went to the library and found books about budgeting and being debt-free. There were so many books to choose from, she wasn't sure what to select. She just grabbed a few and hoped they would help her. After getting home, she popped open a book and started reading. It was LaKenya Taylor's book, *Improving Your Money Flow.* She opened another book, then another. After a while she felt quite overwhelmed with all the information, as she was not an avid reader.

Laura decided to follow the budget plan from the *Improving Your Money Flow* book. She stayed up until midnight to finish her budget.

Never Red: Questions & Challenge

Have you ever struggled with doing the right thing with your paycheck, like paying your tithes at church or paying a bill? How did you overcome it? If you have not overcome it, make a change today.

_____

_____

Was Laura's plan sound? Would you have made the same decision? Was this the best course of action for Laura?

_____

_____

If you've had an issue in this area of spending money hastily, this may be a good spot to stop and answer the same questions that Laura answered (listed below). Your answers may be quite different than Laura's. You may not have answers yet, but still write down thoughts that may come to mind. It is time to make a change and it begins now.

Where did my spending habits come from?

_____

_____

_____

Why am I like this?

_____

_____

_____

What is driving me to want to spend so that I am in bondage to debt instead of being financially free?

_____

_____

_____

What changes do I need to make?

_____

_____

_____

Challenge: *Make a major effort to track your spending for just two weeks (keep receipts); later progress to a month. It is good to do this several times a year to track your spending and to get it in check. It is usually shocking to see how much we spend. Even track your taxes. Many don't see taxes as being a part of their budget, but when you add up those taxes it is alarming what we spend on them. Make it a section in your budget.*

Chapter Seven
Moving Forward

Laura really enjoyed her job. After a month, she knew her way around the building and had met so many nice people. She was feeling good, especially today because it was payday. Laura would receive her first check. Although she was set up for direct deposit, her first payment would come via check. She didn't know exactly what her net amount would be since taxes and insurance would be taken out.

Laura was told that the office secretary dropped off checks at 11:15 a.m. Laura waited patiently, or at least she tried to. It was 11:10 a.m. and she kept her eyes on her computer—more precisely, the bottom right-hand corner where the time was displayed. She waited for the clock to hit 11:15 a.m. It finally did and no check. "Well," thought Laura, "she has to make her rounds. No big deal."

Finally, around 11:20 a.m., Laura spotted the office secretary with envelopes in her hand walking in her direction. Laura turned back to her computer as if she were not concerned. As the office secretary got closer, she began to fumble with the envelopes in her hand and said, "Hi Laura, here's your check."

"Thanks a bunch," said Laura.

Once Laura received her check, she rushed out of the office for a lunch break. As soon as she opened the door to her red car, she called her mom to share in her first real paycheck experience. Laura's mom was all ears.

"Ok, mom, I'm opening it," said Laura as she tore the envelope that held her first big check. Laura's heart was beating so fast, it sounded like there was a drum roll in the background. "Ummmmmm!!!" she muttered as she pulled the check out the envelope. "Wow! $1,050.55!" exclaimed Laura.

Laura's mom was happy for her and congratulated her on her first paycheck. Laura was ecstatic. She rushed off the phone with her mom, bubbling with joy. Laura's mind wanted to wonder off into thinking what she could buy with her first check, but reality was still present. She knew what she had to do. It would be hard, but it would be worth it.

Laura immediately went to the bank where she had banked during college.

As she pulled up to the window, she took out her budget plan and completed a deposit slip with a requested withdrawal of $150. Laura was so glad that she was finally taking responsibility. After a little time had passed Laura heard the bank teller over the intercom say, "Ma'am, have you ever deposited a check from this company before?"

"Well, no, but it's from my place of work," said Laura.

"Ma'am, unfortunately, we will have to put a three-day hold on the check. It's our bank's policy," the teller explained, "so unfortunately, you will not be able to make the withdrawal."

Laura was bummed. She had her plans all set and now things had to change. Laura drove off feeling defeated. "Well, at least I have $30," she thought. The $30 had to last her for three days until her money was released from the bank.

The next day Laura went to work, sat at her desk, and began to log on to her computer. A voice from behind said, "Hi Laura, how are you?" Laura was a little puzzled, as the voice she heard was not familiar.

Laura slowly turned around in her chair with nervous expectation. Laura looked up and said hello to the woman she did not recognize.

"I've heard so many great things about you," the woman said, staring down at Laura. Laura just smiled, not knowing what to say.

"Oh, I guess I should introduce myself. I'm Lisa Hawkins, the director of the accounting department." Lisa extended her hand for a handshake.

Laura threw her hand out quickly to greet Lisa, as she was excited to meet her. Laura had also heard some great things about Lisa, who was well-loved by all departments and was involved in a great deal of community work. Lisa spent a few moments telling Laura about Red Kirk, how it was the best company in the region and how Laura would love it there.

As Lisa spoke, Laura looked at Lisa's features. She was in good shape and carried herself with poise. She held one's attention while talking and had a very strong handshake. Lisa was a confident woman. Laura kept repeating in her mind, "I hope to be as confident as she is one day."

When Laura felt she could get a word in, she replied with excitement, "It's so nice to meet you, Lisa."

"I'm sorry that I'm just getting around to introducing myself. I wanted to check in, see how things were going, how you were settling in," said Lisa.

"I like it here a lot," Laura replied, "everyone is very nice."

"That's great," said Lisa. "I just wanted to say hello. I don't mean to keep you from working. How about we get together for lunch this Friday?"

Laura counted in her head as she thought about when the bank would release her money. "Sure, that would work, what time would you like to go?" Laura asked.

"Will noon work? I can meet you here," Lisa replied.

"Sure! See you then," said Laura.

She was so excited about meeting Lisa and then to be asked to go to lunch with her, Laura could not wait for Friday.

After work, Laura drove past several fast food restaurants. She wanted to stop and get a burger and fries but she knew she couldn't as she had just $30 to last her for three more days. She had food at home, so she went straight there.

Never Red: Questions & Challenge

Have you ever been in a situation like Laura's, where you had to wait on your money for a time? Did it interrupt your plans or did you have a plan B?

_____

_____

_____

How would you have handled only having $30 for three days until you could access your funds? What would you do about food or gas?

_____

_____

_____

Challenge: *Take the $30 challenge. Pick a start date soon and for a whole week limit yourself to $30 to use for lunch for that week. If you don't normally buy lunch, use it for a different meal you normally buy or for all expenses outside of gas during the week. You can do it. Watch and see: your friends, family, or co-workers will probably bother you about going out to eat. If eating out is not your thing but shopping is, limit yourself there. It* *is good to practice self-control. Laura did a good job. You will too.*

Chapter Eight
Lunch with Lisa

Friday finally arrived, and Laura had managed to retain $7 out of the $30 she had. She was not happy about it. Laura walked into the office with her head down, hoping she would not pass Lisa. Laura was so nervous that she even wished Lisa had not come to work or perhaps forgot about the lunch so she would not have to embarrass herself.

Laura went to her cubicle and began to work. Several of her co-workers passed by, saying hello throughout the morning. Each time Laura heard her name being called she thought it was Lisa, but Lisa was nowhere in sight.

It was a few minutes before noon, and Laura's nerves were shot. She started to sweat. All she could think about was how embarrassed she would be if she had to go to lunch with Lisa with only $7 in her pocket. What if Lisa took her to a fancy restaurant downtown or something? So many thoughts ran through Laura's head, but she snapped back to reality when she heard someone walking toward her cubicle. It was Lisa.

"Hey, are you ready to go?" Lisa asked with a smile.

"Oh, hi Lisa, sure I'm ready to go," Laura said as she grabbed her things. She planned to go to the bank after work but really needed to go now since she didn't have enough money for lunch. Laura didn't know how to tell Lisa this without being embarrassed, so she kept quiet.

"How about you meet me downstairs? I'll go get my car and pick you up at the front entrance," said Lisa.

"Sounds like a plan," said Laura as she wiped the sweat from her forehead.

"Did Lisa not want her to drive?" Laura thought. It was something she hadn't even considered would be the case.

Red Kirk was located on the fourth floor of a building that was used by several businesses in South County. As Laura left her cubicle, she greeted several people she was familiar with. When she walked out the front doors of the building, she saw Lisa sitting in a black BMW X5, smiling. Laura was excited to not only see a black car, but a black BMW. When Laura opened the car door she was blown away by the soft leather seats and wood trim on the dash. The glow upon Laura's face was as bright as a headlight cutting through the dark.

"Are you going to get in?" Lisa asked.

"Yes, sorry," said Laura. She got in and fastened her seatbelt as Lisa drove off. Lisa began to ask Laura questions about where she was from, what she enjoyed doing, and many other things, which Laura did not want to talk about.

Soon they arrived at Sicily's, which Lisa said was the finest upscale Italian restaurant in the St. Louis area. Laura didn't mind hearing about the "finest"—it was the "upscale" part that disturbed her. She only had $7.

Lisa pulled into the parking garage directly across the street from Sicily's. Laura's eyes widened at the sign that read "Parking $10 per hour." Laura's eyes roamed, taking in the sights. She was also trying to figure out if she would be able to at least afford a soda.

Lisa and Laura walked across the street and were greeted by the host at the front door of the restaurant. The host was dressed in a black suit and white shirt, which was refreshing for Laura to see until she looked down at what she had on. Laura had on a white top and a blue jean skirt with black Payless flats. In comparison, Lisa wore a black and white pantsuit and a very nice pair of high heels. Laura didn't recognize the name, but they looked expensive.

Laura's mind was racing. "Why am I here? Why did she ask me to lunch? Why don't I have money?"

Laura smiled at the host and followed him and Lisa to their table, which was set with high-quality dishes and silverware. Sicily's, in general, had a great ambiance. It was definitely nicer than her apartment. Laura wanted to stay there—literally.

"I don't know about you, but I'm pretty hungry. Take a look at the menu and order whatever you'd like, my treat this time," said Lisa with a smile.

Laura could have fallen out of her chair upon hearing Lisa's comment. She hoped her relief did not show on her face. Laura opened the menu and winced as she glanced at the prices. It was a good thing Lisa was paying because even if she'd gone to the bank, Laura still couldn't have afforded her meal.

Since Laura had never been to a fancy Italian restaurant, she didn't understand the menu. When the waiter came to the table, Laura waited until Lisa ordered and said, "I'll have what she's having." Laura loved food so it didn't matter what she ate. She knew she would be content, especially with spaghetti. "How can one go wrong?" she thought.

After the waiter walked away, Lisa began a conversation that grabbed Laura's full attention.

Lisa said, "Laura, I wanted to invite you to lunch today to welcome you to the company. I know you've been with us for almost a month and I hope you are enjoying it so far."

"I am," Laura responded.

Lisa continued, "I told Regina, the assistant manager in your department, that she found a jewel when she hired you. I'm aware that you got your degree in business administration. That's a good degree to have. I hope working at Red Kirk will help you meet all your goals."

Laura nodded the whole time Lisa spoke. She was fascinated with how well Lisa spoke, her demeanor, and her confidence. Laura wanted that as well.

Laura began to think again, "Why would someone like Lisa want to take me out to lunch? What do I have to offer?" Out of everything Lisa said, the last statement, "I hope that working at Red Kirk will help you meet all your goals," stuck with Laura.

Laura didn't have goals. Laura had so much going on that she just went from day to day doing what she knew to do. She had no idea she needed to be doing more.

Power Change

Laura was inspired after her lunch with Lisa. As soon as she left work, she went to the bank, withdrew $150, went home, and got started. She thought, "It's time to write down my goals."

Laura pulled out her calendar, a pen, and a notebook. She sat back and thought about what she wanted to achieve not only at Red Kirk, but also for her life in general. Laura began to think about her financial obligations since she now had to pay her monthly rent of $500; her electricity, which fluctuated; her $25 water bill; $303.20 car note; $75 car insurance; and back debt of over $20,000, which included student loans.

Laura wrote out three short term goals to get started:

1. Pay bills on time
2. Work hard at Red Kirk to earn salary increases and be promoted

3. Put at least $100 extra toward old debts

Laura felt a great sense of accomplishment, and she put her notebook down and went to sleep, excited for the day to follow.

Never Red: Questions & Challenge

Have you ever asked these questions: How did I get to where I am today? Why don't I have money? Where am I headed? These are questions I believe many of us have asked before. Don't ever lose your hope. You are on a new road. Jot down a few answers to the above questions.

_____

_____

_____

Laura was full of fear when she knew she was going to lunch with only $7. Limited resources can cause fear and worry to take over one's life. Have you experienced this? How has it affected you? Denounce fear and worry today and embrace peace. God has not forgotten you. Continue to read and see how Laura overcame. You will too.

_____

_____

Are you confident in yourself? Laura was not confident, but she wanted the confidence Lisa had. Have you ever been inspired by someone who had a great deal of confidence? How you were inspired?

_____

_____

Do you have a mentor? If not, get one that will help you move toward your dream. Write down some possible names.

_____

_____

On a scale of 1 to 10, how would you rate yourself with regard to managing your money? Why?

_____

_____

_____

Challenge: *Create three financial goals for this year. (Hint: Goals should include a purpose, timeframe, and dollar amount.) Your goals should be realistic and attainable. For example, buying a $650,000 house within a year, or even five years, on a $30,000 salary would not be considered realistic. If your goal was to pay down a $500 debt within one year on a $30,000 salary, it would be more attainable. Even consider creating a goal board of pictures that represent your goals and look at it often. You can achieve it. Believe and put forth the effort.*

Chapter Nine
The Day After

Laura was feeling good. She finally had her priorities right and was ready to move into a better place financially. Laura wanted to let Lisa know how much she had inspired her. When Laura got to work she found a sticky note on her computer from Lisa, thanking her for going to lunch and letting her know if she needed anything, Lisa would be available.

Laura grinned from ear to ear. One would have thought she had won the lottery. Laura was elated to know that Lisa chose her.

Laura didn't want to waste any time. She decided to go to Lisa and tell her how much she enjoyed their lunch and about the things she learned from their conversation.

Laura had never been to Lisa's office, so she asked the receptionist at the front desk for directions. Lisa's office was on the same floor but on the other side of the building. Laura swiftly walked to Lisa's office and noticed Lisa in an office directly across the hall talking to a co-worker.

Lisa saw Laura out of the corner of her eye and called out, "Laura, go have a seat in my office, I'll be right with you."

Laura did just that. Lisa's office was very executive-looking, decorated with wood panels and nice wall-to-wall windows. Lisa's desk was so clean a dust test would have turned up nothing. Awards and degree plaques aligned the available wall space.

Laura looked on the wall and saw that Lisa had a CPA certificate and a CFP certificate, along with many other degrees. Although Laura knew her title, Lisa hadn't mentioned exactly what she did within the company, so Laura was shocked.

Lisa came in the office and greeted Laura. "What brings you here?" Lisa asked.

"Oh, I saw your note this morning and wanted to thank you for lunch yesterday and share what I learned from our conversation," said Laura.

"Well I'm all ears," said Lisa, smiling.

Laura felt a little nervous since she saw the degrees and certificates on the wall. She was starting to doubt herself again, but thought about how just writing out her goals has changed her for the better. Laura said with courage, "I'm thankful that you took the time out of your busy schedule to have lunch with me yesterday. You don't know how that impacted me. When you said that you hoped that working at Red Kirk would help me meet all my goals you left me with something that changed my view on life. That sparked something in me. I've never written goals before. I went home immediately and wrote down three short-term goals."

    Lisa was thrilled. "Laura, that's wonderful! I hope to inspire so many more to focus not only on their goals, but also their finances," said Lisa.

    "Yes, I see all of your degrees and certificates on the wall, you must know a lot about money," said Laura.

    "Funny you would say that," Lisa replied. "Actually, I didn't gain my financial knowledge through my degrees and certificates, although they did help. I had to make the decision to learn about money to help me become better, and I have it in my heart to help others as well," Lisa said.

    Laura began to see the connection between herself and Lisa. She wondered if Lisa would help her with her situation. Laura had attempted to read books, but reading was not her thing. She thought maybe Lisa could teach her what she knew and assist her in becoming great at handling money.

Laura was nervous about saying anything to Lisa because she was embarrassed about her financial situation and didn't think Lisa would understand. Why would Lisa listen to someone who was in such financial disarray? Laura kept trying to build up her confidence as she continued to listen to Lisa talk about the free financial classes she held within the community in her free time.

In hopes of asking Lisa questions to help her financially, as this was a major part of her goal, Laura politely interrupted, "Lisa, can I ask you something? I'll understand if you say no, but I really need to ask you this. I'm up to my head in debt and I really want to be free from it. I've made attempts but have not stuck with any plan, probably because I haven't had a real plan. I'm just tired of being in the red all the time. I just got paid this week and want to start things off right in taking care of my current bills and old debt. I guess what I'm trying to say is, can you help me?"

There was a brief pause, then Lisa said, "Sure, I'd be willing to help you, but only if you are willing to help yourself by making the changes that are necessary."

As soon as Laura heard this, the light bulb went off and she immediately thought back to when she first met her manager. Mr. Perry said, "Welcome to your place of change." Laura now realized that working at Red Kirk has really been her place of change. If she had not met Lisa she would have remained complacent and not moved toward change.

New Day, New Life

Lisa and Laura set up times to meet during the week to help Laura get on track. Lisa shared so many great tips that she had to ask her to slow it down.

Laura began to learn about boundaries and how her mindset was shaped incorrectly by her parents. Laura's mindset had to be reshaped in order for her to move toward freedom. Laura no longer wanted to model her mom but wanted to model Lisa, a person who took the time to share with her an abundant way of thinking and living. Laura even got to go with Lisa to several of her community events, which sparked a passion in her to help people within her community.

Lisa was also a believer, and they were able to discuss the spiritual aspect of money and its place in the church. Laura found healing from her past with family and the financial failures.

After applying the many tools Lisa gave her, Laura began to see the light and became debt-free within three years. She was promoted within the company several times and she soon left the red world, even Red Kirk. She sold her red car and was eventually able to buy her first black BMW 5 series, debt-free.

Laura decided she would be better off by not having anything red ever again, even though working at Red Kirk was a major blessing.

After eight years of living in St. Louis, Laura decided to move to Mapleton, Nebraska, a place she became familiar with during several business trips while at Red Kirk. The small town and relaxed feel was her main reason for moving, but she wasn't there long before getting involved in her community.

Never Red: Questions & Challenge

Do you have someone to share your financial issues with and get help? If not, do some research and see who may be available in your community or your church. It is good to get help. Also, check for financial literacy classes within your area.

_____

_____

_____

You have to be willing to open up for your financial surgery. You have to be honest. Write down a list of your financial scars (for example, mismanagement, overspending, financial dishonesty and abuse, etc.).

_____

_____

_____

Challenge: *Take the time to write down your fears and hurdles in discussing your financial situation. Also, write down why these things hinder you. It is time to overcome them and focus on your future.*

_____

_____

_____

Laura began to focus on her future. It was time for her to change and she was willing to take bold steps to move forward in change.

You must first:

- *Make a decision*
- *Anticipate a great outcome*
- *Do the work*

  You may fall a few times as you are moving toward your change, and that is OK. Shake the dirt off and get back up and keep going. Your future and the future of your children (if you have them) depend on it. You can do it!

Chapter Ten
The Dress Arrives

Ms. Focuson heard the doorbell. "It must be the dress," she said as she ran down the two flights of stairs to her foyer, filled with beautiful flowers. She could see the delivery man, through the glass paneled door, holding her dress. She was thrilled.

Ms. Focuson happily opened the door and signed for the dress. As soon as she got the dress, she ran upstairs to her closet and tried it on, turning in front of the mirror. The dress was gorgeous. It was a form-fitting dress that hugged her curves beautifully. After her personal beauty show, Ms. Focuson took her dress off and carefully hung in it in the closet in preparation for tomorrow's awards ceremony.

Ms. Focuson's phone began to buzz. She was not sure where her phone was so she followed the sound until she found it on her dresser.

"There it is," said Ms. Focuson, but it was too late; the call went to voicemail.

Ms. Focuson waited a moment then checked her voicemail. As she played her message she heard, "Hello Ms. Focuson, this is Mark Meager. I received a message that you called and would love the opportunity to speak with you about a possible partnership. If Meager & Wilson can establish a working relationship with you and your team to assist our employees and build strategic goals, I know it will not only help our company but also help the community. With the center's assistance, we can avoid situations that led to the workers' strike. I'll be at the Mapleton's Advancement Award Ceremony tomorrow. Perhaps we can chat afterward and then plan a more in-depth meeting next week. Again, I look forward to seeing you and I want to thank you for this opportunity."

Ms. Focuson was glad to receive the call from Mark, as she was ready to move into a new arena of developing programs that would help struggling companies within Mapleton. She couldn't wait to meet with Mark and, more importantly, help the employees at the Meager & Wilson Company.

The Big Day

The next morning, Ms. Focuson went over her speech several times and practiced her walk and her smile. Soon the phone rang. "Who could it be?" she wondered as she rushed to the phone. "I need to leave in an hour."

"Hello?"

"Hi, Laura, this is Lisa. How are you?"

Ms. Focuson sucked in her breath. She would never forget Lisa's voice, but just in case, she asked again, "This is who?"

"This is Lisa."

Ms. Focuson knew for sure it was Lisa Hawkins. She was so happy to hear from her.

Lisa continued, "Laura, I got your invitation to come to your awards ceremony. I want you to know that I'm in town and I will be there."

Ms. Focuson was overwhelmed. She had not talked to Lisa in years and sent an invitation to the last address she had for her. "I'm so glad you are coming. I want to thank you again for everything you've done for me. The time you gave me meant the world to me, and it means so much to have you come to the ceremony. I can't wait to see you," said Ms. Focuson.

"I can't wait to see you," responded Lisa. "Maybe we can catch up after the ceremony."

"I would love that," Ms. Focuson answered.

As Ms. Focuson got off the phone with Lisa, all she could think about were the times they spent together and the help Lisa blessed her with in a time when she had no direction. Also, Ms. Focuson realized that Lisa called her Laura, a name she didn't use anymore because it reminded her of her debt-riddled past. She began to see significance in her first name. Her name no longer represented being in the red, but represented change. Thanks to Lisa.

Laura went through her speech one more time after putting on her black dress and stilettos. She grabbed her black purse and walked down the stairs thinking about her life and how far she had come. Laura opened the front door and gazed at her black BMW that she had always wanted and had finally attained.

She walked slowly to her car and peered back at her lovely home and thanked God for it and for everything that He had blessed her with.

Laura got in her car and smiled, as she was now ready to receive the Mapleton's Advancement Award for her years of service helping to build homes, provide job placement, and teach families how to be financially free.

Never Red: Questions & Challenge
Have you ever accomplished something so great that your old friends would be surprised? How did you handle it? If you haven't, what do you plan to accomplish?

_____

_____

_____

What are some accomplishments that you are proud of? What made you feel accomplished?

_____

_____

_____

Laura was being honored, but as we can see she was still on a mission to help the employees of the Meager & Wilson Company. What is your passion (something that you would do even if you were not paid for it)? Don't delay getting started if you haven't.

_____

_____

_____

Challenge: *Always be thankful. Don't let your situation or where you are today stop you from moving forward. If you stay in the same spot you will remain there. Take a leap forward. If you fall, remember, get back up and keep going. Write down ideas that you have in mind and pray over them daily, asking God for wisdom in how to move forward.*

Laura desired to help people; if that is your desire, start today by getting involved in your community. It is a great thing to help people. Guess what? It is also a great thing to help <u>you</u>. Get educated. Be empowered. You are on your way to freedom.

The End

About the Author

LaKenya Taylor is best known as the "Money Clues Lady" on her husband's *Faith Focus* TV show, where she shares money tips daily. LaKenya has a bachelor's in accounting, a master's in business administration, and is a Registered Paraplanner designee. She has a passion to empower others, both financially and socially. Financially, by providing over 30 free financial classes, as well as teaching a financial literacy class called "Improving Your Money Flow" each semester at a local career and technology center. Socially, by starting Pad It, an outreach program that provides feminine products to women and girls. Over 11,000 feminine products have been donated to Pad It. Pad It covers eleven schools within six cities.

Made in the USA
Lexington, KY
30 July 2017